ADMIT
ONE

AN AMERICAN
SCRAPBOOK

MARTHA COLLINS

PITT POETRY SERIES

Ed Ochester, Editor

ADMIT ONE

AN AMERICAN SCRAPBOOK

MARTHA COLLINS

UNIVERSITY OF PITTSBURGH PRESS

Published by the University of Pittsburgh Press, Pittsburgh, Pa., 15260

Manufactured in the United States of America
Printed on acid-free paper
10 9 8 7 6 5 4 3 2 1

ISBN 13: 978-0-8229-6405-6
ISBN 10: 0-8229-6405-8

in memory of Ota Benga, Carrie Buck,
and countless other victims
of the policies and attitudes
portrayed in this book

and for Pam, Kevin, and Lee
without whom not

CONTENTS

Fair 1

Zoo 19

Fitter 33

Fewer 53

Postscript 75

Acknowledgments 85

ADMIT ONE
AN AMERICAN SCRAPBOOK
MARTHA COLLINS

FAIR

1904 St. Louis World's Fair
Louisiana Purchase Exposition

MEET ME IN ST. LOUIS

OPEN YE GATES
SWING WIDE YE PORTALS
ENTER HEREIN YE SONS OF MAN . . .

My mother went, inside
her mother, mother and father
went in, what did they see?

—

An Ivory City of Palaces
with columns colonnades towers
turrets fountains statues domes

engines working factories farms
dairies bakeries animals art

20 million trees and plants
75 miles of roads and walks
14 miles of railroad track

first electric wall socket
one million electric lights

the most progressed the most—
O Civilization!—the most evolved

—

Don't tell me the lights are shining
Any place but there!

—

900 industries making and selling

hospital schools an underground mine

cablecars railcars automobiles

Schools for Defectives: blind made brooms

                        make

              bring into   being by

              work   trouble   money

              progress   tracks   time

                  for   something out

                  of something

Made / Made of

Festival Hall, w/ gold-leafed dome larger than St. Peter's

    An elephant made of almonds

World's largest organ, w/ over 10,000 pipes[1]

    A windmill made of tools and 5,000 axe blades

Vulcan, world's largest cast-iron statue[2]

    A life-size Teddy Roosevelt on horseback, made of butter

Largest ever rifle, w/ a range of 22 miles

    A 1¼-ton eagle w/ 5,000 feathers, made of bronze[3]

World's largest clock, w/ 13,000-flower face

    A 35-foot King Cotton w/ life-size pickers, made of cotton

World's largest birdcage, w/ walk-through tunnel[4]

    A bear made of 14,000 prunes

The Palace of Art[5]

Current Locations:

[1] Wanamaker's (now Macy's), Philadelphia
[2] Red Mountain, Birmingham, Alabama (still largest)
[3] Wanamaker's
[4] Now in St. Louis Zoo
[5] Now St. Louis Museum of Art

The Pike

Below the Palaces, down
on the Pike, you could Ride

the Shoot the Chute! or watch
an elephant ride it, could Walk

a Street in Cairo! ride a tortoise,
camel or zebra! you could watch

the Boer War reenacted, complete
with Zulus and Bushmen! you

could ride a boat to the North Pole!
or laugh in the mirrory Temple of Mirth

you could go to Dante's Inferno! be
present at the Six Days of Creation

ICE CREAM CONES! COTTON CANDY! HOT DOGS!

Thomas Wolfe, whose mother went to St. Louis when he was four
      to run a boarding house for visitors to the Fair, to which he
      later sent his character-self, whose *mind gave way completely*
      there

T. S. Eliot, who published a high school story based on Fair
      exhibits from the Philippines, about *natives* choosing a king,
      and later created bawdy King Bolo and his Big Black
      Bassturd Kween

Kate Chopin, who collapsed of exhaustion her first day and died
      two days later

Thomas Edison, who arranged electrical exhibits and filmed the
      Pike

An Iowa family, who went for five weeks

My mother's mother and father

Fair / Fair / Fare

religion and trade   in Roman

medieval   to trade or display

or other goods   or animals

county   state   world

free from bias   *doesn't play fair*

beloved woman   completely, quite

clean   spotless   pure

blond   gracious

fair   trade   game   play

the numbers   buy   sell   deal

the not   fair   dark   fare

well   to be   bought   and sold

THE STREET BETWEEN

Because my mother said her mother
Because she said her mother and father

Because I'd always gone to the Fair
in Iowa, sometimes Illinois

Because I'd thought a midway, rides,
cattle and pigs in barns, and they

had those, she said, but more—

But really because I later saw,
with my mother, who lived in St. Louis then,

the Centennial museum exhibit and learned
that people had been brought to the Fair

from Africa, Asia, America (North
and South) to be displayed—

5.2: The Great Louisiana Purchase Exposition opened Saturday. . . . 1:05 was the moment that first saw the flags from thousands of masts mysteriously unfold, the fountains begin to play, and the massive machinery set in motion in response to the touch of President Roosevelt in Washington.

Along the broad avenues and spacious terraces of the great Ivory City representatives of all nations elbowed one another. Tall and gaunt Patagonians walked side by side the Esquimaux. . . . Subjects of the Mikado sauntered along the roadway casting furtive glances at fierce Cosaks; sooty Nubians jostled yellow Mongols, and picturesque Turks, Moors, and Sudanses added rich color to the picture. . . . Of course Europe was represented.

—

9.14: Today's delegation from Du Quoin to the Fair was composed of the following . . .

9.20: The Call acknowledges receipt of an invitation to be present at ceremonies in honor of Illinois Days September 21st and 22nd. . . . The CALL expects to be represented.

—

10.22: [some illegible on microfilm] It should be a matter of congratulation . . . to the section of country of which St. Louis is the metropolitan center that the World's Fair is proving so great a success. . . . Diverse interests, different religions and no religion at all. It has been a task to . . . shape . . . keep . . . within . . . law and order, social . . . moral . . . perilous voyage(s) from their homeland. . . . Sunday closing is being enforced, the fact that it is the centerpiece of a Christian nation is being emphasized

—

11.28: Saturday was another great day at the World's Fair. The Chief Magistrate of this great nation, with members of his family, were viewing the grand and wonderful . . .

ON THE OTHER SIDE

My mother went, inside
her mother, mother and father
went in, what did they learn?

—

Across from the Ivory Palaces
underlined with the strip of the Pike

you could see the Living Exhibits
of the Department of Anthropology
procured by same or Government

in model villages and native dress
(regardless of the weather)

smallest to tallest, lowest
to highest, hairiest, darkest
. . . to *dominant whites*

—

from Patagonia (tallest): 5 males 1 female 1 child

from Japan (Ainu, hairiest): 4 males 3 females 2 children

from Africa (darkest, smallest): 9 males, *including 5 Pygmies*

Ota Benga, Part One

Samuel P. Verner
Acquisition List

> *One Pygmy Patriarch or chief*
> *One adult woman, preferably his wife*
> *One adult man, preferably his son*
> *One adult woman, the wife of . . .*
>
> *. . .*
>
> *Two infants of women in the expedition*
> *Four more Pygmies, preferably adult but young*
> *including a priestess and a priest*
> *or medicine doctors, preferably old*

> —

in the forest, alone, away from the villages:
hunted the elephant, hidden among the trees

teeth filed for   was / was not a
why would they take the tusks and leave the meat?

wife, children killed by neighboring . . .
no, by Leopold's *Force Publique*

for *a pound of salt and a bolt of cloth*
Verner bought Ota Benga (exhibit one)

leafwork and forest shadow
dancing with the forest, with the moon

dancing for (*because they like it*)
dancing for, in place of— *for the trees*

—

Verner: *an extremely interesting little fellow*

—

displayed in "village" with four other "Pygmies"

Most Startling Ethnological Exhibit

bows and arrows hunting horn spears

half-human, a false start

anthropometricists measured, proved

brain size small, approaching the Simian

Artiba   Otto Bang   Autobank

the Lesson of Your Race

—

*The only genuine African cannibal
in America today*   (was / was not a)

*the only human chattel. . . . He
belongs to the Exposition . . .*

—

Exposition *to the Pygmies:*
  Cash and Gifts, $8.35

Indian Village: After the Purchase

from the US (many from 1803 acquisition):
over 400, from numerous tribes

in earth lodge and prairie-
grass hut, in tipi hogan longhouse

posed performed made and sold
only *native* clothes songs art

canoes cradles baskets beads
blankets moccasins pots

Pawnee Arapaho Wichita
Dakota Lakota Navajo . . .

and the Fair's most famous
exhibit, Geronimo

—

And beyond the Villages, up
the hill, at the highest point

on the grounds: a Model Indian
School for *successfully developed*—

farming husbandry harness-making
laundry classes cooking for girls

a representation of . . . human development
from savagery . . . toward enlightenment
as accelerated by association and training

A visitor: *They're the* dearest *little things*

Philippine Reservation: After the War

from the Philippines (from 1898 acquisition):
nearly 1,200 in six villages, four groups

NEGRITOS (lowest, smallest, darkest)
    the true savages   missing link
    monkey-like   (could become extinct)

IGOROTS (including Bontocs, most warlike)
    spirit-worshippers   headhunters
    almost naked   danced   ate dog

MOROS (more intelligent)
    colorful clothes   *picturesque*
    but *fanatical*   *Muslim*   *fierce*

VISAYANS (highest)
    Catholic church   theater   school
    Western dress   *beautiful*   skilled

. . . and non-tribal Scouts and Constables
    from the Spanish-American War:
    highest grade   result of American rule

. . . and also a school
    Such advancement and in so short a time
    said President Theodore Roosevelt

THE FAIR'S LARGEST EXHIBIT

Physical Culture

Then came Anthropology Days
when *primitive* people competed against
each other in *civilized* athletes' games

while registered athletes competed
in the Third (modern) Olympics

stronger of limb
fleeter of foot
clearer of eye
far more enduring

not to mention other competitions
congresses dances parades

and a college-credit ethnology course
taught by Professor Frederick Starr
using the human exhibits

The white man can do more and better
than the yellow, the yellow . . . than the red or black

W. G. McGee, Chief of Anthropology
Louisiana Purchase Exposition

Exposition / Expose / Exposure

setting forth   an ex-

a present   position   point

act   of exposing   state

of being   exposed

displayed   disclosed

wares   details   laid open

disposed   of former   opposed

for want   of shelter   warmth

a surface   laid open

to view   revealing   *a northern*

to light   public   indecent   fact

of being   without

as they are now, our ancestors were

Good night, my Fair, farewell

ZOO

The Bronx, 1906

St. Louis Zoo

went with my mother
my father my first
zoo when I was seven:

bears riding bicycles, lions
and tigers, elephants standing
on two legs, *the world's*
largest birdcage

—which in fact was the cage
built for the Fair which the city
bought to launch the zoo
which opened in 1910

Ota Benga, Part Two

more people there than palm trees here and
elephants in cages   make them play tricks

said Ota Benga said Samuel Verner
who took the Africans back to the forest

and traveled for 18 months to gather
artifacts animals plants and also

(licensed by Leopold) ivory rubber—

and meanwhile Ota Benga's new wife
was killed by a snake no family no tribe

                    said Verner more or less

—

So Verner took him back to New York
to the Museum of Natural History where

he hoped to sell his chimpanzees snake
his beetles artifacts plants and where

he arranged for Ota Benga to stay
which he did until he misunderstood

the director's gestures (chair → woman)

or understood and still threw the chair . . .

Madison Grant, Part One

hunter friend of Theodore Roosevelt
helped create national forests and parks
for hunting, but then   *for the trees*

helped save the bison, preserve the redwoods
helped save eagles   antelope   whales

to leave   a country   with trees
on the hillsides   beasts in the forests
fish in the streams   birds in the air

and after the hunting, before the parks, before
the book that would make him (in)famous

conceived the Bronx Zoo

—

conceived because the animals
he hunted were disappearing

not the usual zoo with cages
but something *entirely divergent*

four times larger than even Berlin's
animals living *as in the wild*

fund-raised organized hired planned

beaver dam   bear den   bison prairie

Zoo

zoo-   logical   garden   plant

an antelope elephant tree

zoo-   logical park   as in

enclosure meant   for game

for us we parked

the car could leave

Elephant

hidden among the

village children had never seen

why would they take the tusks and leave

poisoned arrows   big game guns

line of elephants   line of men with tusks

—

father of animals
mountain of meat

—

plowed fields   felled logs   cleared roads   hauled goods
hunted tigers   carried men   in processions   into battle

—

Leopold   ivory   pianos   slaves
to carry   quotas   hands   cut off
to prove   bullets   tusks   cut off

—

jumbo (*adj.*, huge) from
Jumbo, African elephant, brought . . .

—

Jumbo, brought by Barnum, skeleton of:
Museum of Natural History, 1889

Topsy, electrocuted 1903, Coney Island:
device made, event filmed by Edison

Gunda, Asian, arrived 1904, Bronx Zoo:
performed, attacked, was chained, shot

Congo, African, arrived 1905, Bronx Zoo

performers, divers, drivers, the disappearing
one with Houdini, Hippodrome Theater, 1905

    —all except Topsy seen by Ota Benga, 1906

    Whipping an elephant does not hurt him;
        but he thinks *that it does.*

William T. Hornaday, Director, Bronx Zoo

Ota Benga, Part Three

Then Verner took his poisonous snake
his chimpanzee to the Bronx Zoo

and also took Ota Benga who
would have a place to stay

—

So Ota Benga arrived at the Zoo,

its woodlands, its range for the buffalo

(but no buffalo), its court, its walks, its sea

lion pool, its house where the elephants lived

(but no trees), its house where the primates lived

(but no trees)—and there was Verner's

chimpanzee, and an orangutan named Dohong

who was dressed in Western clothes and poured tea

—

And then he was housed in the Primate House

where he hung his hammock and wove his nets

and watched the orangutan try to escape

and then they put up a sign:

> The African Pigmy, "Ota Benga."
> Age 23 years. Height 4 feet 11 inches.
> Weight 103 pounds. Brought from the Kasai River,
> Congo Free State, South Central Africa
> by Dr. Samuel P. Verner
> Exhibited each afternoon during September

and the people came and the *New York Times* said:
BUSHMAN SHARES A CAGE
　　WITH BRONX PARK APES
　　　　their heads are much alike

and zoo director Hornaday said:
Madison Grant gave *full approval*
　　We are taking excellent care
　　　　He has one of the best rooms
　　　　　　in the primate house

—

And a German visitor asked: *Ist das ein Mensch?*

And a woman asked if she could buy him

—

Then black ministers raised a protest, went
to Hornaday, then to the Mayor, then to Madison Grant,

and at last the sign came down, Ota Benga was free to roam
the grounds, but still the visitors came, 40,000 in one day:

they chased him . . . poked him . . . tripped him up

—

was *attached to* they said was

employed by they said was

exhibited said the sign

—

they chased him	he shot an arrow
they poked him	he brandished a knife
they tripped him	he tried to take off his clothes

—

this *well-developed little man*
this *normal specimen of his race*

—*this untamed ebony bunch of bother*
said Hornaday and let the ministers

take Ota Benga to live in the Colored
Orphan Asylum in Brooklyn and then

on their farm on Long Island and then
on a farm where he was paid and then . . .

Animal / Anima

all of us   all but us   only

(but not us) the mammals   or only

us: *animal in us*   or only

the male of us: *brute*

no *animals*   in the Bible

only *beasts*   as *of the field*

not *us:*   it says   *breathed*

into   in our image   of the dust

anima breath   to *anima*

soul   but all animals

breathe the   same   it's one

long song   the same   air

Relatives

Bronx Zoo Primate (Monkey) House
with MONKEYS carved on the lintel:
opened 1901, closed 2012

now gorillas longurs lemurs baboons
in separate *natural* habitats

no monkey cages trikes to ride
no chimpanzee orangutan no

> *abba dabba dabba dabba dabba dabba dabba dabba*
> *said the monkey to the chimp . . .* (1914)

African rainforests   beds in trees
leaves for scoops   leaves to bathe

> *In 2007, 1,300 chimps in US labs for research*
> *including inoculation with infectious agents*

In April 2014, seven
chimpanzees escaped
from the Kansas City Zoo

broke a log from a fallen tree
leaned it against a wall
climbed up and over

Missing / Missing

person   animal   escaped from the

species   chance   target   goal

day at the   monkey house

closed   regretting   absence

dressed like   kept undressed

we who dress   undress are missing

longing   not even a near   a hit

we   are the missing   link

FITTER

Where They Lived

Du Quoin, Illinois, 1916

My mother and father were twelve.
She went to the Baptist Church, he went
to the Christian. They went to the Ward
School. They lived on one side

of the railroad tracks. On the other
side lived Negroes, who went to a Negro
church and school, and Irish German Polish
French, who went (mostly) to the Catholic.

My mother's father was German, my father's
mother Swiss-German and Irish (they thought
the Irish English), but they themselves were not
immigrants who'd lived on the other side.

Ota Benga, Part Four

. . . he went to live in Lynchburg, Virginia

where Anne Spencer (African American poet) befriended him
where Carrie Allen McCray (African American poet) was born 1913

where he lived with McCray's family
studied in the Baptist Seminary
worked in a tobacco factory

where he got his filed teeth capped
and was known as Otto Bingo

. . . and spent time in the surrounding woods

where turkeys squirrels and rabbits
where he gathered roots and honey
strung his bow and shot his arrows

where he taught young boys to hunt and fish
and danced again *for the trees*

where he pulled the caps from his teeth
and died beside his fire, his arrows by his side,
his own bullet through his heart in 1916

—

Verner: *one of the most determined little fellows that ever breathed*

McCray: *You gave us more / than we could ever give to you*

Madison Grant, Part Two

from conserving wildlife for hunting to
preserving (*for the trees*) the forests to
managing wildlife (kill the unfit) to

—

As anthropologists said, there were three or four
    the white . . . than the yellow. . . than the red or black (McGee)
But there were three within the white
    Nordic   Alpine   Mediterranean
Not a new idea (see Ripley, 1899) but Grant
    popularized *Nordic* (the term) and

added race to *eugenics* (a word
invented by Darwin's cousin Galton)
which was already leading to segregation
and sterilization of *the unfit,* for

The Passing . . .
    see *race suicide* (a term invented by Ross
    and adopted by Theodore Roosevelt)

The Passing of the Great . . .
    the *Nordic* the strong the virile the tall the blond

The Passing of the Great Race (Scribner's, 1916)

Race / Race

stock   strain   family   line

breed   blood   skin   shape

of the head   of the pack

animal   human   judge

better   fitter   swiftly

to find   foot   horse   car   run

for your life   around

town   the block   the camp

to the top   the finish   contend

compete   in   for   against

the other   the not so

great   not even in the

Better Babies

In 1911, the Iowa State Fair, which was one of the country's
    oldest agricultural and industrial expositions,
which used the same grandstand, some of the same cattle swine
    sheep and poultry barns and pavilions I saw as a child,
which had featured an Indian village, high-diving horses, bicycle
    races, and in 1896 had staged its first locomotive collision—

in 1911, the Fair featured the Wright Brothers, the first of its cows
    made of butter (famous when I was a child and even now),
as well as its first Baby Health Contest, conceived by physician
    Florence Sherbon and PTA leader Mary T. Watts,
who had asked: *You are raising better cattle . . . horses . . . hogs,*
    why don't you raise better babies? And so:

In 1911, babies were measured for height, weight, *anthropometric*
    traits and mental development, and advertised and displayed,
in an automobile in the Fair's Parade, as *Iowa's Best Crop.*

By 1916, when the Fair's lawns were mowed by sheep
    and the first 4-H Club Baby Beef Contest was held,
most states had Better Baby Contests, many co-sponsored
    and advertised by *The Woman's Home Companion,*
which conferred certificates and prizes on winning babies.

In 1911, Charles Davenport published *Heredity in Relation to Eugenics*
    and urged Sherbon and Watts to score *50% for heredity.*
In 1913, Watts reported to Davenport that *Eugenic Expositions*
    were often associated with the contests,
and by 1920 the women had helped Better Babies evolve
    into Fitter Family Contests, also held at state fairs.

PROGRAM FOR BABY HEALTH WEEK GIVEN

May 7 Baby Sunday. Appropriate sermons in all the churches.

May 9–12 Better Babies Contest! Scientific Scoring of Children. . . . May 13 Mass meeting . . . the highest scoring children will be announced and prizes awarded.

—

ELECTION ON SEGREGATION

2.29: St. Louis voters today are deciding by ballot whether negroes here shall be compelled to live within residential districts selected for them. The segregation bill . . . would prevent whites and negroes from living in the same blocks.

—

SEGREGATION WINS 3–1

THE BIRTH OF A NATION
MARCH 1916
Pittenger Theater, Centralia
Eighth Wonder of the World
Sherman's March to the Sea, The Burning of Atlanta, The Rise of the Ku Klux Klan . . .
500 Scenes   10,000 People
9,000 Horses   Cost $50,000

NEGRO LYNCHED IN ST. CHARLES, BURNED IN BARN

—

HOUNDS TRAIL ITALIAN SLAYER

—

BOARD MAY TAKE BABY FROM ITS INSANE MOTHER

4.12: The state . . . will decide what to do with the two months old baby of Mrs. Lottie Wilson, inmate at the Lincoln state school and colony. The child was sent to the institution with its mother . . . but there is no evidence that it is feeble minded. . . . The fact that this feeble minded woman has had four children is cited . . . as proof of the need of the law requiring the commitment of all feeble minded in the state. The law went into effect last July.

GO TO CHURCH ON SUNDAY

TRAINED TO FORGET TRAITS
600 RED CHILDREN BEING TRAINED IN WAYS OF WHITES

4.18 Chilocco, Ok. The government is endeavoring to efface from the minds of Indian boys and girls all memory of their ancestors and primal traits.

Some Eugenics

Marriage selection / large
families encouraged for the fit

Legal prohibition of marriage
by the unfit: the feeble-minded epileptic
indigent inebriate insane in 30 states by 1914

                    —*but the unmarried*

Legal segregation of the feeble-minded etc.
in asylums training schools colonies

                    —*but the expense*

Legal sterilization of
in 15 states by 1916

*the prime duty, the inescapable duty, of the good citizen of the right type
is to leave his or her blood behind him. . . . We have no business
to permit the perpetuation of citizens of the wrong type.*
(Theodore Roosevelt to Charles Davenport, 1913)

In 1916, Stanford's Terman revised the Binet-Simon test
which Henry Goddard had translated and used since 1908
and for which he invented the word *moron* (from Greek, *dull)*
for the *feeble-minded,* the *high-grade defectives.*

In 1917, Terman used the test to determine officer fitness
and after the war tested school children, finding mental
deficiency high among Mexicans, Negroes, Italians.

How did the little . . . Why did the little . . .
What did the little moron say . . .

In the 1917 film *The Black Stork,*
Dr. Harry Haiselden—Illinois surgeon
and practitioner of *lethal eugenics,* who had refused
to perform surgery on a number of *defective* newborns—
played a version of himself refusing to save such a child.

What are believed to be divine laws and a sentimental belief
in the sanctity of human life tend to prevent the elimination
of defective infants and the sterilization of such adults
as are themselves of no value to the community.
The laws of nature require the obliteration of the unfit.
(Madison Grant)

In 1880, Harry Laughlin was born in Iowa.

Later he lived in Kirksville, Missouri, where he graduated from and
taught at the Kirksville Normal School, the college where I
first taught (now Truman State University).

In 1910, he was hired by Charles Davenport to supervise the
Eugenics Record Office and help train social workers to
interview *defective* persons in mental institutions, hospitals
for epileptics, prisons, orphanages, circus midways.

In 1915, he called for the ultimate sterilization of *the lowest ten
percent of the human stock.*

In 1939, dismissed from his position, he returned to Kirksville.
Seizures revealed that Laughlin was an epileptic.

—

In 1911, Iowa passed its first sterilization law, which applied to
*criminals, idiots, feeble-minded, imbeciles, lunatics, drunkards,
drug fiends, epileptics, syphilitics, etc., moral and sexual perverts,
and diseased and degenerate persons.*

Between 1910 and 1963, Iowa sterilized 1,910 persons, 1,574 of them
while I was being raised / going to school / living in Iowa.

In 1979, the Eugenics Board of Iowa was abolished.

Geneses

genus before   *genesis* from   trans-

lated from   In the beginning   was good

before *genetic* before   *eugenics*

made up to be   even better   before

miscegenation made up   from *mixed*

with *genus* as if   there were separate

from anti-Lincoln   in 1864   which

also sounded   like nation

Meanwhile

Meanwhile miscegenation laws in 30 states mostly
anti-Negro-and-white plus bills proposed and defeated
but also Chinese-Japanese-Mongolian-Indian-
Hindu-and/or-Filipino(*Malay*)-and-white

In 1915 *The Birth of a Nation* was shown
in the White House to Woodrow Wilson
who may or may not as reported have said *all*

so terribly true but who in 1913 had re-
segregated federal agencies offices facilities
dismissed Black workers or put them behind screens

Meanwhile hundreds of thousands
of Blacks arrested on the way to *stop*
for nothing more than on the way

fined what could not pay made
to sign or mark to sign away
back to railroad field mine

chained locked enslaved
again signed away by white
paper white X on black

In 1915 *The Birth of a Nation*—seen by thousands, banned
in some cities, followed by protests, riots in others—
broke all box-office records for decades to come

In 1915 *The Birth of a Nation*
led to the rebirth of the Ku Klux Klan

Meanwhile segregation laws for train cars   streetcars
trashcans   schools   libraries   bathrooms   poolrooms   books
hearses   graveyards   prisons   circus tickets   telephone booths

In 1915, 56 African Americans were lynched,
including William Stanley, who after being
castrated was burned alive over a two-

hour period during which he was lowered
into raised out of lowered into etc. a fire, after

which photographs of the event appeared
on postcards, one with the message:
This is the barbecue we had last night

Cross

The cross between a white man and an Indian is an Indian;
the cross between a white man and a negro is a negro;
the cross between a white man and a Hindu is a Hindu;
and the cross between any of the three European races
and a Jew is a Jew.

Madison Grant

—

The cross between a eugenicist

and anyone is unlikely:

neither Francis Galton nor Madison Grant
nor Harry Laughlin nor Henry Goddard
nor Harry Haiselden

had children of his own.

Alien, Part One

If you were Chinese, you had (mostly) been excluded since 1882.
If you were Japanese, things were complex after 1907–8.

If you were anything else, you were not excluded as such in 1916

although there were many who thought you should be
if you were the eastern or southern European
that you increasingly were: Russian / Polish
Jewish   Italian   Polish   Slavic   Greek . . .

—and you could have been excluded as a convict
lunatic   beggar   pauper   polygamist   anarchist
prostitute   epileptic   contract laborer   mental defective
bearer of loathsome / contagious disease . . . : a growing list.

If you came after 1892, you probably (90%) arrived on Ellis Island,
where in 1906 you were still likely (99%) to be admitted,

but where, if you came in 1914, you might have been given
an intelligence test by Henry Goddard, the results of which
were inconclusive (and your chances of being excluded small)
but in 1916 you might (10%) have been marked X *mental defect*.

If you came in 1917, the new Immigration Act could have excluded
you for 33 reasons, and for the first time would have done so
if you could not pass a literacy test (for which Madison Grant
had lobbied) or if you came from an extensive *Asiatic Barred Zone*.

If you were admitted, you might have taken a train
from New York to southern Illinois, where you probably
would have worked in a mine, especially if you were Italian.

Fitter Families

Yea, I have a goodly heritage my mother
said her sister said the Bible said
and it does and they did we do but

that was also the motto of Fitter Families
for Future Firesides, contests featured
at state fairs using anthropometric

measurements medical dental vision
exams intelligence tests personality
evaluations of families some

with several generations as well
as eugenic family histories. The forms
had a blank for *race* (which could be *Nordic*)

and charts were posted with literacy rates
for NATIVE-BORN FOREIGN-BORN NEGROES
as well as birth rates for NATIVE-BORN ALIEN

There were also displays with flashing lights

> This light flashes every 15 seconds
> O
> Every 15 seconds $100 of your money
> goes for the care of persons with bad
> heredity such as the insane, feeble-
> minded, criminals & other defectives.

—and medals awarded to winners, which read:

YEA, I HAVE A GOODLY HERITAGE

Fit / Fit

healthy   hearty   worthy   made

to fight   explore   rule   a good

fit for a   fit the facts

to be   fit   as befitting

un-   diseased   defective   dragging

down   might have a   right

here in the yard   to be tied   so can't

have more   of them   select

fit into a   square   a round

of weeping   anger   and starts

to be stopped   before   they throw

a poor   poor   and if the shoe

Carrie Buck, Part One

was born in 1906   her father died or left   her mother
Emma to charity   put in foster care   with the Dobbs

in 1910 the year[1]   the Virginia Colony for Epileptics
was founded   near Lynchburg   *an act of kindness* they

said and sent her to school   to the sixth grade   *very good*
deportment / lessons   but withdrew her   to help with chores

endless work she said but sang   in the choir   *good days*
and bad she said   *a good girl* she said   but still a tomboy

in 1914 the year the Colony added   the *Feeble-Minded*
to its mission and name   and 1916 the year Superintendent

Albert Priddy began to freely   sterilize women   afflicted
he said   with *pelvic diseases*   in the Colony where   in 1920

Emma   accused of immorality   (had two more children)
and prostitution   was taken by Dobbs   and admitted

where she was tested   and found despite   reading and
writing excellent penmanship   to be   a *Low Grade Moron*

Colony where   she would live until   she died where
in 1924   her daughter Carrie   would also be admitted

---

[1] Also the year Ota Benga moved permanently to Lynchburg

to be continued unless

discontinued

FEWER

—— 1924 ——

What They Were Doing / What They Did

Du Quoin, Illinois, 1924

My mother and father were twenty.

She was teaching second grade
in the (all-white) John B. Ward School.

He was working in Jones Drugstore
and joining / had joined / would (briefly) join

the Ku Klux Klan, which was appearing that year
in local churches with gifts and commendations.

Her father was cited for contempt of court
for criticizing, in his newspaper, the release

of a white man and a Negro woman convicted of
a brazen violation of the laws . . . and of common decency.

He reported the citation in the headline story
(A. W. ESSICK ORDERED TO JAIL) and *accepted responsibility*

the same day the paper announced that the President
had signed into law the new immigration bill.

Madison Grant, Part Three

After *The Passing of the Great Race*

    which was cited by scholars, ministers, politicians
    the Ku Klux Klan and Margaret Sanger—

    which influenced (among others) Edgar Rice Burroughs
    and Lothrop Stoddard (*The Rising Tide of Color,* 1920)—

    which appeared in four editions, the last and largest
    in 1921, all edited and commended by Maxwell Perkins—

after *The Passing,* Madison Grant

    presided over / co-founded / co-directed
    most of the major eugenics organizations

    created / inspired / was essential to immigration
    reform, including the 1924 Immigration Restriction Act

    conceived / achieved Virginia's 1924 Racial Integrity Act
    campaigned with Marcus Garvey for Negro repatriation

    —and devised an ingenious plan to save the redwoods
    which were threatened with extinction, like the great race.

After *The Passing of the Great Race*

    which was published in Germany in 1925, Adolf Hitler
    (who owned a copy) wrote (according to another eugenicist)
    a letter to Madison Grant that said: *The book is my Bible.*

Parodists

"Civilization's going to pieces," broke out Tom violently. "I've gotten to be a terrible pessimist about things. Have you read 'The Rise of the Colored Empires' by this man Goddard? . . . Well, it's a fine book, and everybody ought to read it. The idea is if we don't look out the white race will be—will be utterly submerged. It's all scientific stuff; it's been proved."

F. Scott Fitzgerald, *The Great Gatsby* (1925)

He was a white man, but he knew when he had enough. After all the white race might not always be supreme. This Moslem revolt. Unrest in the East. Trouble in the West. Things looked black in the South. Now this condition of things in the North. Where was it taking him? Where did it all lead?

Ernest Hemingway, *The Torrents of Spring: A Romantic Novel in Honor of the Passing of a Great Race* (1926)

Alien, Part Two

1921 Sacco and Vanzetti convicted

    Italian   immigrant   anarchist

1920–22 Henry Ford buys   publishes   weekly
newspaper   with anti-Semitic columns   compels
dealers   to buy   placed   in new cars   made
into pamphlets   into languages   into German

    no civilization   no great achievement
    in any realm but the realm of "get"

1920 Madison Grant courts Albert Johnson   Chair
of House Immigration   recommends Harry Laughlin
who testifies   is appointed   Expert Eugenics Agent
to Congress   Grant works with Johnson   who tells
Congress   US Consuls anticipate   1 million Jews

    abnormally twisted   unassimilable   filthy
    un-American   often dangerous in their habits

1921 Grant lobbies   publicizes   creates with Johnson
one-year   Emergency Quota Act   which decreases
immigration allows   each nation only   3% of its 1910

1922 Harvard President Lowell announces quota for Jews

1922 Emergency Quota Act extended for two years

Pass / Pass / Pass

through   over   across

the river   gate   way to the

other   side   world   onto

one's issue   the torch   the next

slip   away   of paper   a test

into or onto   or into a law or

off one's self   as something   other

than what   because one couldn't

came to   such a   by on the other

side   or over   fallen   all under

standing   without   not in

not from   not on

Carrie Buck, Part Two

was 17 in 1924 had been *assaulted*
she said by Alice Dobbs' nephew

> *hallucinations* the Dobbs said *outbreaks* she
> was/was not an *epileptic* pregnant she

was *a good girl* she said

> was *morally delinquent* the Dobbs said she
> would go to the Colony after the baby
> the Dobbs would keep the baby

—

After being sued by an angry husband
Superintendent Albert Priddy sterilized only
for Colony patients' relief he said but inspired

by Harry Laughlin's Model Sterilization Law
he urged and aided the writing of a law
for Virginia which passed the same day

in 1924 that a strengthened miscegenation
law to *preserve racial integrity* also passed.

—

In June 1924, Carrie Buck, who had completed
the fifth grade, joined her mother Emma in the Colony

> where Albert Priddy found her to be
> *feeble-minded* of the *lowest grade Moron class* a
> *moral delinquent* who had borne *a mentally defective child*

—

moral delinquents are
mental defectives are
moral delinquents are
mental defectives

—

In July the Colony Board approved the sterilization
of Carrie Buck, a test case for the new law,

for which Priddy appointed (1) Aubrey Strode,
who'd written the law, to represent the Colony, and

(2) a guardian who appointed a former Colony Director
and boyhood friend of Strode to represent Carrie.

—

Assisted by Harry Laughlin, Strode prepared the case

which stressed heredity   mother Emma   Carrie
herself whom witnesses did not know but of whom

and daughter Vivian of whom a social worker said
seems not quite a normal baby . . . a look about it

and presented also two doctors two eugenics
experts   *to decrease defectives   to save expense*

including, by deposition, Harry Laughlin
feeble-mindedness   moral delinquency   social inadequacy

The lawyer representing Carrie made few objections,
presented no evidence, called no witnesses.

—

The judge approved the sterilization, a decision appealed
(as intended) with John Bell replacing the now-deceased Priddy.

The appeal failing (as intended), the case went, as *Buck v. Bell*,
to the US Supreme Court (as intended), which in 1927 upheld

the ruling, 8–1, the majority opinion written by Justice Oliver
Wendell Holmes: *Three generations of imbeciles are enough.*

Racial Integrity

In 1923, Virginian Earnest Sevier Cox,
inspired and helped by Madison Grant,

published *White America,* in which he proposed
the gathering of Negroes in concentration camps
to be followed by their deportation to Africa.

To return the favor, Cox followed Grant's lead and
(aided by Dr. Walter Plecker and composer John
Powell) used Grant's work to create and pass,

the same day as Virginia's Sterilization Act,
its 1924 Racial Integrity Act, the most strict
anti-miscegenation law in the country.

The original version prohibited marriage between
non-whites and *whites,* the latter defined as people
with *no trace whatsoever of any blood other than Caucasian.*

But the protest of a legislator with distinguished ancestry
led to the "Pocahontas exception," whereby people
with 1/16 or less of *Indian blood* were still white.

> *The lower never has been and never can be*
> *raised to the level of the higher.*
> (Walter Plecker)

For over twenty years, Dr. Plecker, Registrar of Vital
Statistics, pursued non-whites through birth, death

and tax records, as well as through *living informants,*
barring marriages, removing children from white

schools, exhuming bodies suspected of having
been wrongly buried in white cemeteries,

classifying all Indians as non-white
(declaring all to have negro blood),

and urging other states to adopt similar
laws, as Georgia and Alabama soon would do.

> *If the purity of the two races is to be maintained,*
> *they cannot continue to live side by side.*
> (Madison Grant)

At the 1923 Texas State Fair, the imperial wizard
of the Ku Klux Klan praised Madison Grant
as a man *of great education and mind.*

Later he said: *we are pleased that modern research
is finding scientific backing for [our] convictions.
We do not need [it] ourselves; we know we are right.*

Marriage

When my mother and father decided to marry in Illinois, they
   could have done so even if one of them had been . . .

When my just-married mother and father moved to Texas, they
   would have ceased to be married if one of them had been . . .

When I was young, my mother was sure her daughter would never
   want to marry . . .

When I met my first husband, my father said *But he's Irish, the Irish*
   lived on the other . . .

When I married my first husband, we had to pass a Wassermann
   syphilis test or we could not . . .

When I told the doctor I didn't want children, he said, *But you must*
   have children.

Carrie Buck, Part Three

In October 1927, Carrie Buck was sterilized at the Virginia Colony.

In November, she was discharged *on furlough* to work for a family.

In 1928, her sister Doris, 14, was sterilized at the Colony.

In 1932, Carrie married her first husband, joined the Methodist
church and sang in the choir.

The same year, her daughter Vivian Dobbs, 8, who was once on
the school honor roll, died.

In 1965, Carrie married her second husband.

In 1974, Virginia repealed the Compulsory Sterilization Act.

In 1980, Carrie said: *They just told me I had to have an operation.*

In 1983, Carrie Buck Eagle Detamore died.

something   done   caught in the

out   up   upon   perform

an operation   piece   part

pretend   as if   nothing

lost   doing   ayes

have   it will not   do   due

to them   behave   as if   unto

first   were not   final

Alien, Part Three

Then Madison Grant met with Congressman Albert Johnson
again to devise a formula for the 1924 Immigration Act,

which was based on the earlier census of 1890 (when there
were fewer immigrants from eastern and southern Europe),

thus reducing to 12% the influx of Jews, Italians, etc., from
a pre–World War annual million to (as it turned out) 20,000.

Seven eugenicists testified, including Harry Laughlin,
who in 200 pages of testimony cited analyzed Army IQ tests

with Nordics on top, Jews on the bottom, and said the formula
would favor Nordics over *non-essential members of the community.*

Grant, too ill to testify, wrote that the *scientific and just* formula
would keep out *lower types* who could *displace native Americans*

and wrote an article targeting immigrants as *criminal   insane*
while the *Saturday Evening Post* and *NY Times* argued for passage.

Suddenly, said an opposing congressman, *a new word made its way
into the English language—Nordic, Nordic—everywhere you turned.*

But the Eugenicists lobbied congress members, *bombarding*
them with letters   telegrams   telephone calls   —and after a long

debate on a clause excluding the Japanese (which led a Japanese
publicist to predict *eventual collision on the Pacific*), the bill passed.

Once We Were

once we were immigrants
given to thought we were
given the right to be
taking what wasn't our
making what wasn't
who wasn't us were

—

take take take
off your shoes your taken
from shoes your take
down shoes your
shoes on the table
your take—

—

table the con-
versation the talk the
top of the table steeple
sky for just a minute be
quiet listen: the shifting
crumbs on the table

—

shiftless we said the
shifty eyes gave them
away we didn't see
the less than dress
a shift a slip as in
under another shaft

—

shaft to have to hold
an arrow handle for hammer
column to build a shaft
of light our enlightened
missile we own the whole
mine we own the shaft

—

mine! we could not stop
the baby *mine!* we would
not stop ourselves mine
it drill it strip it right
down to hear us making
taking over taken out

—

stop for a listen for
once we were may be our
getting forgotten a shifting
to taken mistaken to get
set for the coming all
hands on the table

March 21: "The Birth of a Nation" is finally to be exhibited in Du Quoin. . . . There is nothing in the picture to offend. . . . Any race has undesirable members . . .

—

April 1: What the editor has to say . . . will possibly offend some. . . . The one thing that is doing more to keep the colored race from progress . . . is the wily, crooked politician. . . . About all that is necessary to vote the colored population . . . against any one man is the statement that he is a member of the Ku Klux Klan.

—

THREE ITALIANS ARRESTED FOR MAKING LIQUOR

—

May 23: The pastor of the Sunfield Methodist Church was presented with a purse and a note of appreciation at a special service by 30 robed Klansmen. . . . [The speaker] commended the new immigration measure which cuts down the number of aliens . . . admitted yearly, and explained why it was necessary to stem the tide of immigration if this nation is to survive.

—

SCIONS OF RICH JEWISH FAMILIES CONFESS THEIR GUILT IN MURDER

June 2: . . . a powerful sermon-lecture upon the virus that today confronts America. "Militant Christianity . . . is the only hope. . . . America's greatest danger is from aliens whose moral standards are lower than ours, whose religion tolerates practices outlawed by American churches, and from a comparatively small clique of financiers whose only faith is greed."

AMERICANS WANTED TO JOIN THE KU KLUX KLAN
If you are American born, white, Gentile, Protestant, and of good character, you are eligible!
America Is In Danger—

Sept. 6: The ministers of Herrin today declared the only way to stop bloodshed and lawlessness . . . was continued activity by the Ku Klux Klan. "I am going to warn my congregation," said the pastor of the Christian Church, "that they must stand by the Klan. . . . However, the foreign population is sneaky and must be watched."

—

KLAN MEETING ATTRACTS SEVERAL THOUSAND HERE

Re-enactments

In 1923, Will R. Hayes, my mother's sister's father-in-law-to-be,
    apparently inspired by his visit to the 1904 St. Louis Fair,
    founded and opened his own fair in Du Quoin.

In 1924, the Du Quoin State Fair featured Joe Mendi, *the $100,000
    chimpanzee, who . . . does a Paderewski on his own piano, enjoys a
    Havana perfecta, dines at table, is fond of dress clothes.* (*Du Quoin
    Evening Call*)

In 1925, Joe Mendi played his piano and drank Cokes at a drugstore
    lunch counter in Dayton, Tennessee, throughout the Scopes
    trial.

—

In 1924, John Cromartie, a Scottish man, applied to live in the Bronx
    Zoo, *in a cage between the Orang-outang and the Chimpanzee,* as
    an *educational exhibit.*

In 1924, David Garnett, son of translator Constance Garnett,
    published a novel in which a man successfully applies to live
    in a cage in the London Zoo, between an orangutan and a
    chimpanzee.

In 1992, artists Guillermo Gómez-Peña and Coco Fusco locked
    themselves in a cage and presented themselves as aboriginal
    inhabitants of an island in the Gulf of Mexico. Nearly half
    the visitors who viewed them in museums and arts festivals
    believed the two were "real" "native" "captives."

bearded lady   bird girl   pinheads   giant
woman   tiny men and women   armless
woman   legless armless human torso   man
with three legs and two . . .   conjoined twins

—

The 1932 film *Freaks* featured most of the above
(some of them playing themselves) taking revenge
on their ("normal") tormenting would-be killers.

—

In 1931, Michigan outlawed *the exhibition of any*
deformed human being or human monstrosity,
except as used for scientific purposes.

—

The Third International Eugenics Conference (1932)
included a photography exhibit of often-naked residents
of Letchworth Village for the Feeble-minded and Epileptic.

—

cretinism   albinism   mongolism
microencephaly   epilepsy   delinquency
dyschondroplasia   flaring ears

Admit / Admit

one   two   them   it

was a right   wrong   just

the ticket   members   only   into

the country   school   bar   refuse

hate to   have to   concede

as evidence   into the record

we have to   guilt   mistake   own

as a right   openly   into

POSTSCRIPT

Postscript One

1920s–30s American eugenicists report on / publish / review
German / German report on / publish / review American

> *Germany has awakened to the importance of increasing
> its proportion of pure Nordic blood.* (Madison Grant, 1928)

1925–26 In *Mein Kampf,* Hitler cites US Immigration Restriction Act

> *I regard Henry Ford as my inspiration.* (Adolf Hitler)

1933 German Law for Prevention of Hereditarily Diseased Progeny
modeled on Harry Laughlin's Model Sterilization Law
with nine similar categories for the *Hitlerschnitt:*
almost 400,000 sterilized in four years

> *The Germans are beating us at our own game!*
> (Dr. Joseph DeJarnette, who testified against Carrie Buck)

1935 Nuremberg Laws make Jews non-citizens
forbid marriage or sexual relations between citizens and Jews

> *The laws against miscegenation must be greatly extended
> if the higher races are to be maintained.* (Madison Grant)

1936 Heidelberg University awards honorary doctorates
to Harry Laughlin and Robert Foster Kennedy of Cornell
who advocates euthanasia for feeble-minded children under five

> *the utterly unfit . . . nature's mistakes* (Kennedy)

1939 German euthanasia program begins for defective newborns
then defective children to 3, then 8, then 12, then 16—then adults
already sterilized, but seen as *unnütze Esser* ("useless eaters"):
killed by injection or gas chambers (disguised
as showers) and burned in crematoria

> *To keep a mentally ill person costs . . . 4 marks a day. There are 300,000*
> *mentally ill people in care. How much do these people cost to keep?*
> (Nazi school curriculum)

1939 Lothrop Stoddard meets eugenicists and officials, including
Hitler, during four months in Germany, and writes that Nazi law

> *is weeding out the worst strains in the Germanic*
> *stock in a scientific and truly humanitarian way.*

1939 Wagner-Rogers Bill—endorsed by Eleanor Roosevelt—
to admit 20,000 refugee children from Germany dies in committee

> *20,000 charming children would all too soon grow into*
> *20,000 ugly adults.* (FDR's cousin Laura Delano Houghteling)

1941–45 6 million Jews and millions of others exterminated
some with equipment used for mental defectives

> Nuremberg Doctors Trials Defense
> cites US immigration / miscegenation / sterilization laws
> quotes Madison Grant, and Oliver Wendell Holmes in *Buck v. Bell*

Postscript Two

Meanwhile   increasingly   from 1930s to
1970s   sterilization of   non-whites especially

women   some during   childbirth   fewer
in institutions   more on welfare   doctors
wouldn't   treat pregnant unless   they agreed

But they were mis-   or not informed
told *appendectomy*   told *reversible   health*

In California   a third of all US cases   dis-
proportionate number   of Spanish names

In North Carolina   twice as many   as whites
from 1930s when Aid to Dependent   to non-whites

Of Native American many   maybe a fourth

In Puerto Rico   a third of all   world's highest
percentage   explicitly economic   *la operación*

Fewer legal   but more and more   in deep South
in Alabama   African American sisters   ages
14 and 12   without consent   in 1973   a year after

the Tuskegee Untreated Syphilis Study   begun in 1932
using uninformed African American men   was ended

—not to mention   how many unreported   extra-
or illegal   welfare threatened   sign or you won't

Scrap / Scrap / Scraps

bit   part   discarded   old

useless   torn   from scrape   rip

into pieces   get into a   over

a thing   cut   out   from us

him   her   fragments   save

as in paper   words   unlike

waste   can have   significant

something   out of   something

Postscript Three

Can't feed 'em? Don't breed 'em
—Bumper Sticker, 2014

Abort it and try again. It would be immoral
to bring it into the world if you have the choice.
—Richard Dawkins on Twitter, after being asked
about a fetus with Down syndrome, September 2014

The United States is being invaded. And the Obama administration is
welcoming the invaders with open arms. It's beyond frightening to
imagine that our own government has unleashed this kind of evil on our
streets. And heaven forbid, these illegals harm our wives and children.
—Todd Starnes, Fox News, March 2014

You put me in charge of Medicaid, the first thing I'd do
is get Norplant, birth control implants, or tubal ligations.
—Russell Pearce, Arizona Republican
party vice chair, September 2014

Illegal aliens with communicable diseases and conditions such as
tuberculosis, scabies, and head lice are entering our country unabated.
There is a very real security risk to Americans.
—flyer for National Day of Protesting against Immigrant
Reform, Amnesty, and Border Surge, July 18, 2014, CNN

communist-raised, communist-educated, communist-nurtured
sub-human mongrel . . . Barack Hussein Obama . . . a chimpanzee
—Ted Nugent, January 2014

Exit / Exeunt

take   the nearest   last   off

to the left   stage   show   over

a marked   door   line

visitor   handler   exhibit

with animal   guarded   the barred

banned   with child   without

all of them   gatherers   gathered

or some of them   citizens   justices

unfit   excluded   except

closed   no   or into the open

air   the way   out   will

not be   the way   we came

ACKNOWLEDGMENTS

I am deeply grateful to the Radcliffe Institute for Advanced Study for its support of 40 Concord Avenue, which gave me the space and time that allowed much of this book to be researched, pondered, and written.

My personal thanks to Ilya Kaminsky, who suggested that I might be writing a trilogy long before I thought of this book; to Pamela Alexander, Kwame Dawes, Rachel Kadish, Daniel Okrent, Kevin Prufer, and Lee Sharkey for reading, encouraging, suggesting, correcting; and to Ed Ochester and the wonderful staff at the University of Pittsburgh Press.

My thanks as well to Jan Perone and the staff of the Abraham Lincoln Presidential Library in Springfield, Illinois, for access to and help with the archives of my grandfather's newspaper, the *Du Quoin Evening Call*.

The sources I read, consulted, and viewed are too numerous to mention, but the following (in addition to others identified in the text) were essential or at least useful for specific topics and sections and, in many cases, influenced me in general ways as well.

I should note that although I have not consciously invented factual material, I have not attempted to resolve differences among sources. Quotations (in italics) are, by intention at least, accurate, except for a very few omissions of single words or ellipses.

On the 1904 World's Fair: The centennial exhibition of the 1904 World's Fair at the Missouri History Museum provided the initial impetus for this book, and subsequent visits to the Museum contributed to it; the Museum's website (http://mohistory.org) has also been an essential resource. Also Nancy J. Parezo and Don D. Fowler, *Anthropology Goes to the Fair: The 1904 Louisiana Purchase Exposition* (2007); Robert W. Rydell, *All the World's a Fair: Visions of Empire at American International Expositions, 1876–1916* (1984); Joe Sonderman and Mike Truax, *St. Louis: The 1904 World's Fair* (2008); James Gilbert, *Whose Fair? Experience, Memory, and the History of the Great St. Louis Exposition* (2009); the film *The World's Greatest Fair* (2004); and the archives of the Washington University Library in St. Louis, for access to T. S. Eliot's high school story. The title of and the two lines quoted near the beginning of the first section of this book are from the popular 1904 song "Meet Me in St. Louis, Louis."

On Ota Benga: Phillips Verner Bradford and Harvey Blume, *Ota Benga: The Pygmy in the Zoo* (1992). Also the documentary films *Ota Benga: A Pygmy in America* (2002) and *Human Zoo* (2009), as well as sources for the 1904 Fair, listed above, and the biography of Madison Grant, listed below. Two important books were published after I had completed the Ota Benga sections: Carrie Allen McCray's very moving book of poems, *Ota Benga under My Mother's Roof* (2012), and Pamela Newkirk's impressively researched and documented *Spectacle: The Astonishing Life of Ota Benga* (2015). I am indebted to McCray for some details in "Ota Benga, Part Four," and to Newkirk (whose book was published just as this book was going into production) for a few last-minute changes and omissions that were prompted by her excellent work.

On the Bronx Zoo, zoos: Exhibits at the Bronx Zoo; William Bridges, *Gathering of Animals: An Unconventional History of the New York Zoological Society* (1974); also Robert Delort, *The Life and Lore of the Elephant* (1990). David Garnett's novel is *A Man in the Zoo*, reissued with *Lady into Fox* (1928; 1985).

On Madison Grant: the excellent biography by Jonathan Peter Spiro, *Defending the Master Race: Conservation, Eugenics, and the Legacy of Madison Grant* (2009), which also contributed to more general discussions of eugenics, immigration, and miscegenation, as well as Grant's own *The Passing of the Great Race* (1916) and other selected writings. Related primary sources: Lothrop Stoddard, *The Rising Tide of Color against White World-Supremacy* (1920) and Earnest Sevier Cox, *White America* (1923).

On Carrie Buck: Paul A. Lombardo, *Three Generations, No Imbeciles: Eugenics, The Supreme Court, and Buck v. Bell* (2008); J. David Smith and K. Ray Nelson, *The Sterilization of Carrie Buck* (1989); and Stephen Jay Gould, "Carrie Buck's Daughter," *Natural History* (July 1984).

On eugenics: Harry Bruinius, *Better for All the World: The Secret History of Forced Sterilization and America's Quest for Racial Purity* (2006), which I read with great interest some years before I began this book; also the excellent archival websites of the Cold Harbor Spring Laboratory, www.dnalc.org and www.eugenicsarchive.org. In addition: Diane B. Paul, *Controlling Human Heredity, 1865 to the Present* (1995); Paul A. Lombardo, ed., *A Century of Eugenics in America* (2010); Laura L. Lovett, *Conceiving the Future: Pronatalism, Reproduction, and the Family in the United States, 1890–1938* (2007);

Gregory Michael Dorr, *Segregation's Science: Eugenics and Society in Virginia* (2008); Edwin Black, *War against the Weak: Eugenics and America's Campaign to Create a Master Race* (2003); Daylanne K. English, *Unnatural Selections: Eugenics in American Modernism and the Harlem Renaissance* (2004); Steven Selden, "Transforming Better Babies into Fitter Families: Archival Resources and the History of the American Eugenics Movement, 1908–1930," *Proceedings of the American Philosophical Society* 149, no. 2 (June 2005); Jessie Spaulding Smith, "Marriage Sterilization and Commitment Laws Aimed at Decreasing Mental Deficiency," *Journal of Criminal Law and Criminology* 364 (1914); Lutz Kaelber, "Eugenics: Compulsory Sterilization Laws in 50 American States," http://www.uvm.edu/~lkaelber/eugenics/.

On miscegenation: Peggy Pascoe, *What Comes Naturally: Miscegenation Law and the Making of Race in America* (2009), and Elise Lemire, *Miscegenation: Making Race in America* (2002), as well as several sources mentioned above under eugenics.

On immigration and race: Roger Daniels, *Not Like Us: Immigrants and Minorities in America, 1890–1924* (1997); Oscar Handlin, *A Pictorial History of Immigration* (1972); Vincent J. Cannato, *American Passage: The History of Ellis Island* (2009); Thomas F. Gossett, *Race: The History of an Idea in America* (1963); Maldwyn Allen Jones, *American Immigration* (1961); David Robert Schreindl, "Sowing The Seeds of War: the *New York Times'* Coverage of Japanese-American Tensions, A Prelude to Conflict in the Pacific, 1920–1941" (MA Thesis, Brigham Young University, 2004); and Grace Abbott, "The Immigrant and Coal Mining Communities of Illinois," *Bulletin of the Immigrants Commission, State of Illinois* (1920).

On Nazi Germany: In addition to a number of the texts mentioned above, Stefan Kühl, *The Nazi Connection: Eugenics, American Racism, and German National Socialism* (1994); Timothy W. Ryback, *Hitler's Private Library: The Books That Shaped His Life* (2008); and the website http://www.history learningsite.co.uk/Nazi_Education.htm.

Finally, I would like to thank the editors of the following publications, in which some selections from this book first appeared: *Alaska Quarterly Review, Copper Nickel, Michigan Quarterly Review, Plume, Poets.org, Poetry International, Prairie Schooner, Salamander,* and *Solstice.*